GOD'S GIFTS:
SPIRITUAL WRITINGS

A Book of Inspirational Poems, Prose, and Quotations

By

Frederick Douglas Harper

ISBN: 1-4107-7074-5 (e-book)
ISBN: 1-4107-7075-3 (Paperback)
ISBN: 1-4107-7076-1 (Dust Jacket)

Library of Congress Control Number: 2003094928

This book is printed on acid free paper.

Printed in the United States of America
Bloomington, IN

1stBooks – rev. 07/31/03

ACKNOWLEDGMENTS

Firstly, I thank God, the Greatest Spirit of all time and existence, for giving me the gift of being a positive messenger of good through my written and spoken words. Secondly, I acknowledge and thank my dear mother, Reatha M. Harper (1922-1985), a naturally spiritual person of good heart and prophetic vision, who was there for me in spirit and physical presence throughout her motherly years on Earth.

I am also thankful to numerous persons who have encouraged my writing or helped promulgate my poetry at various points during the past 18 years. Among these persons are Nap Turner who has consistently read my poems on Washington, DC area's WPFW 89.3 FM Radio for the last 15-plus years, and Hodari Ali who sold my book, *Poems on Love and Life*, in his Pyramid Bookstore for more than 10 consecutive years. Others who have played a significant role in helping to publicize my poem books are Pearl Breland, Mattie Carey, Mozella Carter, Sherri Council, Brenda Crawford, Kenneth A. DeSandies, Peola Butler Dews, Edna Downey, Bernadine Duncan, Dolores Finger-Wright, Richard Hadley, Frederick V. Harper, Jacqueline A. Harper, F. Yvonne Hicks, Lillian Holloman, Pam Middlebrook, Laura Qa, Bettye J. Robertson, Ida Ross-Johnson, Ellie Saifnoorian, Paul W. Smith, W.O. Stone, Herbert and Iona Striner, and Sylvia Walker. These persons have helped me in significant or sustained ways such as getting bookstores to adopt my books, sponsoring poetry readings and book signings, telling their many friends about my poems, and buying bulk copies of my poem books to give to others as gifts on special occasions. To these persons and others who have helped and encouraged me along my way, I acknowledge you and say to you that I am very grateful and appreciative.

Regarding this book in particular, I express my gratitude to Melissa Hinkson who proofread the first draft of the manuscript and provided valuable feedback to me. Furthermore, I acknowledge two persons, Allyson Sharp and Tracy Wiggins, who encouraged me to finish the manuscript and get *God's Gifts...* published. I am especially thankful to Tracy for providing the graphic artwork for the front cover of this book. A spiritually gifted person, Tracy, as a youth, received a vision of the image that appears on the front cover of this book. After drawing the vision from her mind's image, she received a psychic message that in the future she would find out what to do with the drawing. After reading the unpublished manuscript of *God's Gifts...*, Tracy unselfishly gave me the gift of her artwork, stating that I was meant to have it and use it with this book. Tracy had interpreted the abstract figures in her drawing as dancers. However, when I first saw the artwork, I immediately perceived the figure in the middle of the image as a spirit ascending to heaven and the two outer figures as spiritual guides or angels. To me, the abstract artwork also has symbolic meaning for each person who chooses to follow a spiritual path of goodwill on Earth and, in doing so, is protected by God's spiritual guides as well as helped by numerous human beings along that path—a path of growing as a human being and giving back to others.

TABLE OF CONTENTS

PROSE ON

SPIRITUAL BELIEFS

Frederick Douglas Harper

ON BEING SPIRITUAL

Prose 1

To be spiritual is simply to be aware of one's purpose and meaning; not necessarily to be better or pious or aloof from common living, but to be natural, constructive, giving, loving, sharing, warm, peaceful, purposeful, growing, appreciative, and totally aware of Earth's sacred life and natural beauty.

To be spiritual is to have a healthy respect for the sacredness of life and the sacredness of the cycles, balances, and perpetuity of life so destined by God's guiding Great Spirit. To be spiritual is to have a respect for the sacredness of God's universal energy; energy that is so destined by God's creations within and of Himself.

To be spiritual certainly is to be appreciative of a God-given talent, to use that talent for good, and to hone that talent to the highest. To be spiritual, certainly, is to be humbled by one's fortunes as well as one's pain and misfortunes, to be humbled by one's human frailty as well as oneself as an ephemeral being or as God's earthly flower in bloom.

To be spiritual is to give unselfishly of oneself for the welfare, growth, and happiness of others, especially for the nourishment of the young and the well being of the old.

To be spiritual, surely, is to be totally and constantly aware of and thankful for God's existence and presence around and within us from day to day and in every way.

ON THE ESSENCE OF GOD'S SPIRIT
Prose 2

God is one and only, whole, all existence, and everything. We can never know God in this human life, but we can feel God's presence through spiritual energy. God is neither anthropomorphic nor finite, but exists, I believe, as a whole, as one whole that is expanding with time. God speaks to us through the energy of earthly guardian angels of the present and divine spirits of earthly lives of the past. Earthly angels are human beings, I believe, who have both power to "watch over" and to communicate divine messages as conduits of God's divine spirits. Divine spirits of God, I believe, can receive messages from and send messages to human beings who are anointed with special gifts of divine destiny—whether persons use those special gifts of divine destiny depends on whether they adhere to and follow divine messages intended for their reception.

Those anointed to receive God's grace of message are conduits of his spirits; conduits who are simply persons with a divine destiny to help and positively influence humanity. Earthly angels can be destined to meet persons for whom they are to protect, assist, or magnify; and, in doing so, are enhanced themselves in these same ways.

God is divine in working through the energies of other entities. God can work in us and through us with or without our awareness of our choices and actions.

I BELIEVE IN GOD'S GIFT
Prose 3

I believe that God has blessed me, through His earthly guardian angels and His celestial divine spirits, to be a conduit of word and verse, to be a messenger gifted to inspire and guide, to be a shepherd of good and truth of it. I believe because I have been so fortunately blessed to do so, that is, with little effort of my mind's thought and with much great fulfillment of a gift realized and shared. For the gift of being a giver, I thank God for His guardian angels and divine spirits and for their messages to me and messages through me. As I thank my God, I also thank my earthly guardian angels who have guided my life and path, as well as the divine spirits that watch over me and inspire my thoughts from day to day. I have borne my appreciation for good fortune through my constant prayerful thoughts and words as well as through my good deeds.

I thank God for the joy and peace of my journey in life as a gift of His continual divine grace upon me, and I pray in daily thought that others will see their paths as clearly as the day has been laid before them and as clearly as the light in which they have been gifted and blessed to walk, if they so choose.

I believe that if we walk life's path of developing our gift and sharing its fruits, we will be blessed to receive the blessings that divine destiny can bestow upon our hearts and souls; we will be instilled, I believe, with a spirit that will make good of us and our gifts to the world.

ON PEACE
Prose 4

Personal peace is a state of mind, a state of body, and a state of attitude. It comes with how one sees the world and reacts to it. Personal peace, unlike agitation, comes with experience as well as a state of balance of one's own organism, one's self. A person who is at peace with self is one who has often overcome much of the worldly fears, as well as personal guilt. Peace can be found not just in one's thought of peace but in one's experience of complete tranquility of being. It is often achieved and maintained by:

❖ Not permitting others to disturb one's state of balance,

❖ Finding solitude and quiet as a time for peace within oneself,

❖ Slowing down and being aware of oneself and one's surroundings,

❖ Rehearsing peaceful meditative states in one's daily life,

❖ Listening to one's mind and body for agitation or imbalance, and positively addressing one's needs,

❖ Negotiating with one's loved ones for harmony and peace,

❖ Allowing peace to come spiritually into one's heart through positive thoughts and feelings,

❖ Ignoring, as much as possible, the malicious and destructive thoughts and actions of others, and

❖ Allowing the spirit of God's energy to permeate the core of one's life and to move one toward good for self and others.

MY WISH

Prose 5

My wish in life as a poet is for my work to live in appreciation with the life of the human race, and that my spirit will live, beyond my life on Earth, in the central meaning and heart of my work as God's work and as God's gift.

My humble wish of life this day is to arrange words and sculpt verse that say much to help the human race to make Earth a better place.

MY PURPOSE AS A HUMAN BEING
Prose 6

I feel that I have been anointed as a conduit of God's spirit, and thus I have accepted this in thought and action as much as I could. I have sought not to seek a title as such, but rather simply to share my blessings and gift, and to strive for the simple things in life: to "grow" and "give back" and to procreate life in love while helping to raise and nourish the young.

ON SPIRITUALITY AND RELIGION
Prose 7

I believe that our religion should be a spiritual way that is exemplified by our way of living, our attitudes, and our actions toward ourselves, others, and the world we know. I believe that one who is truly religious is one who has little to no guilt, anxiety, anger, or hatred—one who is truly at peace with self and God. I believe that our true church or temple should reside within our hearts, our good thoughts, and our positive way of life.

I believe that death is a stage in the development of spiritual energy of a person. The quality of our life on Earth will determine the quality of our spiritual energy and thus our "life" beyond Earth.

I believe that spiritual energy beyond can communicate with life's energy on Earth, but the opposite is very limited unless we cannot realize or receive confirmation for the Godly thoughts or spiritual messages we send. Certainly, it seems that we can know things without knowing that we know, and such knowledge can influence our earthly energy and actions.

GOD'S SPIRITUAL POETRY
Prose 8

P oetry is the sculpting of words into messages for the purpose of evoking thought, emotion, and action. It serves as the inspirational torch that burns deep in hearts and minds. Divine poetry is destined; it does not come from the mind of the ambitious, but from a divine source of energy as communicated through one who is chosen with the simple talent of being a spiritual conduit of ideas, images, thoughts, feelings, and meaningful spiritual messages. Inspirational, consoling, and healing poetry comes from God's spirits as assigned to the chosen pen that chooses to write.

MESSAGE TO THE YOUNG
Prose 9

If I can say anything to make a positive difference in the life of the young, I will when I can. What I will likely say and what I can say with some wisdom of experience and insight are:

1. Develop a talent given you as God's gift to the world,
2. Work hard at that worthy God-given talent,
3. Take risks to achieve and contribute in an arena worthy of making God's Earth a better place,
4. Control excesses and impulses or surely they will distract you, if not destroy you,
5. Waste little time in combating the anger and foolishness of others, except, on rare occasions, to protect a reputation built and deserved or to safeguard the innocent self and others from harm,
6. Find a good reason or more for which to live or surely death may find a liking to you,
7. Eat to live and not live to eat, because the latter will serve as your reason for being,
8. Exercise regularly, drink enough healthy liquids, and enjoy peaceful relaxation between periods of meaningful, hard work,
9. Find quality time to spend with family or loved ones in your life, while learning to give love and receive love,
10. Accept kindness and gratitude with appreciation, and give with joy in the absence of expectation or anticipation,
11. Above all, try to do what is naturally and spiritually right for yourself and the welfare of deserving others.

SIMPLE RULES OF LIFE
Prose 10

1. Love those who deserve and accept your love, and avoid those who can do harm to you and your loved ones.

2. Do not destroy sacred life or beauty any more than necessary for survival and the perpetuity of your life. A single life is sacred, but more important is the life of a single species or group, and, even more important is the life of Earth itself.

3. The destiny of life's passage on Earth, as we know it, is eventual death of species as new ones evolve and the eventual transformation and death of Earth as a living celestial body. Our overall purpose, therefore, should be to preserve and enhance God's Earth and life on Earth.

4. Greed is a universal crime that should be abhorred in every form and contested in every way. Selfishness is the driving force of greed, and, therefore, should be discouraged.

5. Giving is more important than receiving, for through giving are we renewed to give again and to receive more abundantly.

6. To lose a life or love is not necessarily to grieve for such but rather to realize that we have been blessed to have had, to have known, and to have experienced something precious and of great value.

7. We cannot own anyone or anything; we can only share or temporarily appreciate precious things, because all things created and acquired on Earth are eventually lost, transferred, or transformed.

SPIRITUAL PRAYERS
AND
MEDITATION

Frederick Douglas Harper

A HUMBLE PRAYER

My God, all praise to Thy Great Spirit and presence.
My God, all thanks for what I have experienced in Thy
Sacred space and time.
    Let me continue to be in harmony with my energy;
    Let the remaining course of my life run the divine
        Destiny of good will;
    Let my continual thoughts of Thy presence and creations
        Be witness to my prayer;
    Let my good deeds, wherever, be testimony to my faith;

From day to day, give me:
    The patience to listen,
    The wisdom to understand,
    The unselfishness to defer my own needs,
    The insight to realize my potential and purpose,
    The will power to be growthful and productive,
    The courage to face unknowns,
    The thoughtfulness to give and humbly receive,
    The capacity to love and be loved,
    An openness to accept my human vulnerability,
    A habit toward responsibility,
    A penchant for hard work,
    A respect for self and all that is sacred and good,
    The strength to control destructive urges,
    The ability to be modest in the face of good fortune,
    And the propensity to be at peace with myself.

AMEN.

Reprinted: Harper's *Poems on Love & Life,* 1985.

A DAILY PRAYER

Oh God, on each morning's wake,
Teach me to appreciate light's day;
And with each action of success and good,
Always remind me to do what I should;
>   To keep my feet on the ground,
>   My body and head sound,
>   And my eyes on a purpose found;

To know always that You are everything
And that I am just one thing;
Great Sacred One of all, accept my daily
Thoughts of appreciation for Your blessings
Bestowed and a rededication to
>   Your spirits' call;

Prevent me from hiding my talents in
Cowardice or basking too much in the
>   Light of success;
Give me the strength to stay my pace
And journey Your race unknown but shown
By Your light and love from day to day.
>   AMEN.

Reprinted: Harper's *Romantica: On Peace & Romance*, 1988.

A PRAYER OF FORGIVENESS

Oh God,
As we sit here as one,
Bless this our family and its members—
To relieve the burden from our hearts,
To relieve the hurt
That pains and separates us;

Lift our tension,
To be replaced by calm and peace;
Come so serenely
Into each and all of our hearts,
And breathe forgiveness
Of another and each other;

Teach us to speak of kindness, and
To disdain evil thoughts forever;
Be with us and around us—
Blessing us as one,
Blessing us as a family
From day to day.

AMEN.

A PRAYER FOR THE HUMAN SPECIES

Gracious spirits divine of past,
Beseech our dear God
That we as a species will last,
And make of good our precious
Gifts of mind and hand;
That Earth will become a better place,
And we as a human race
Will not lose face;

Great spirits of God,
We pray through you, that our
Dear God will bless us too;
Grand spirits of God and yore,
We pray through you that our
Dear God will bless us more;

And if we die as a species can do,
We pray that our spirits will shape
Earth's life anew.

AMEN.

A BABY SHOWER'S PRAYER

God as Whole, God of us all;
God of our angelic spirits known;
Accept our appreciation on
This occasion as celebration of life;
The most precious gift from You.
Teach us to realize our purpose as we live;
    To create and nourish life itself, and
    To grow and give of ourselves.
Accept so humbly our gratitude of
Daily gifts from You:
    The air we breathe, the water we drink,
    And the food that nourishes us.
Bless our love as Your union,
And accept our thanks for Your gift
Of ourselves to each other;
Bless the life we have created in
Our baby, and guide this life
    As Your unique gift.
Bless all our loved ones who are here today—
Each as Your unique creation, all as
Special people whom we value in life;
Bless the children here and those who
    Care for them.
In Your very precious name we offer this prayer,
    AMEN.

A MAN'S PRAYER

Great God of all, humble us as men before
Your omnipresent Spirit, and accept us as
The seeds of Your precious human life;
Lower our heads to honor You in praise—
For Your divine creations of us and all that
Stems sacred from You.

As grandfathers, fathers, and keepers of life,
We beg of You dear God to accept our
Prayerful thanks for the good You allow us to
Do and attempt to do for and with our sons,
In trying to help them to become worthy men in
Your sight and worthy travelers of Your path.

We pray that You will open our hearts to the
Way of humility, and temper the arrogance and
Anger that arise in us from time to time;
Dear God, bless our hands to create for
Good, and condemn the hands of destruction
That can drive us to ways of ill will.

Teach us, we implore, to honor Your name
By honoring our women as the very sacred
Temples of Your life reproduced; teach us

(continued)

20

To raise our young in the ways of right,

And in the way of a deference for their elders

Who care for them and care about them;

Teach us the way of honesty and hard work,

And guide us in Your light of responsibility,

Love, self-pride, and decency; teach us to love,

Respect, and care for our families; teach us to

Respect worthy others as we should respect

Ourselves, to love worthy others as we should

Love ourselves, and to abhor greed and selfishness.

Our dear God, we beg of you to

Purge the war-like urge to slay from our very

Souls, and lead us to ways of rightness as role

Models for our daughters and sons who

Look up to us; we pray to You dear God

To remind us as men to love our fathers and

Our grandfathers, and to honor the men who helped

Us to become men; always make us mindful to

Remember those men who perished before us—

By accident, battle of war, or other circumstance.

(continued)

Direct our hearts and spirits toward a way of
Tolerance and benevolence, and away from that
Of intolerance, hatred, and wrongful destruction;
Teach us, from day to day, to trust, appreciate, and
Work with our fellow brothers toward survival and
Security for ourselves, our families, and the global
Community in which we live;
Make us ever mindful to respect and love our
Daughters, wives, mothers, grandmothers, aunts, and
Other dear loved ones.

Give us the courage to live for good cause, and
Not to kill or die as an excuse for pain and power;
Oh God, give us the wisdom to do right and the
Courage and good strength to do our best;
Shear and sear all evil from the marrow of our
Bones, and endear our souls, minds, and muscles
To a way of caring for all life and a righteous
Giving of ourselves.

In Your precious name and spirit, as men,
We humbly pray.

AMEN.

A SUPPER'S PRAYER

Oh benevolent Spirit of God,
Hear us and accept our humble prayer;
Great and noble God of us all,
Accept our appreciation for your divine greatness
And the Gift you have given us as life itself;
Accept our praise of You as
Giver of all the good we are and do;
Be ever gracious in accepting our thanks
For this food as the substance of life, and
For the water and good drink that sustain us
From day to day;
Bless our family as a unit and bless each
Of us here today as your creation;
Bless the less fortunate to be fortunate,
And the very fortunate to help the unfortunate;
Bless all those among
The human race of Earth as You bless the
Homeless of the world;
Bless the young and the old, bless the
Endangered life of Earth and those
Who protect and nourish the living;
As we eat now in love and good spirit,
Bless us to be forever appreciative of
Your gifts from day to day.
　　　AMEN.

A TABLE PRAYER

As we sit around
Your gifts of life,
We humbly pray
Our praise of You.
Oh dear and gracious God,
We beseech you to
Accept our meager
Prayer of thanks for Your
Great blessings of this our
Table's gifts;
Keep us together, and
Bless us forever,
To be healthy and happy
In your light;
Nourish our bodies,
And breathe strength
Into our bodies and souls;
In your most precious
And benevolent name,
We pray to You,

AMEN.

FOR THE UNBORN

A thought, a prayer—
For a life unrealized;
A thought, a prayer—
For an arrow plucked in flight,
For a rosebud picked at dawn;

Talents gone unknown, and
Undeveloped images never to be
Appreciated;
A baby disowned and a child unknown,
A seed energized; a seed minimized
To dismemberment;

A thought, a prayer—
For a life unrealized,
For a life that is no more.

Reprinted: Harper's *Romantica: On Peace & Romance*, 1988.

Frederick Douglas Harper

GOD'S GIFTS

Frederick Douglas Harper

GIVING IS A GIFT

There is no joy like
That of giving for the joy of it;
Because giving is a gift
In and within itself;
There is no more of a
Joy than one's gift
Of self to another or others,
Or part of one's self as with
Talent shared and time spent;
There is no more of a
Joy than a gift given
By God and used once
Developed, and
Developed for its sharing
As God's gift;
So give without condition,
And receive without expectation.

THE GREATEST GIFT

That greatest gift is the
  Joy of a gift shared;
That giving of ourselves,

    Our time,

    Our support,

    Our services,

    Our talents;

That greatest gift is the giving

Of ourselves to a worthy other,

So that special one can enhance

The value and number of his or her

    Gifts to the world.

So let us give and spread

Our love and joy by giving through

The gift of ourselves to another;

Let us be blessed by the satisfaction

Of giving so that we can receive

The greater gift of renewed fortune

To give once more of ourselves.

From: Harper's *Romantica: On Peace & Romance*, 1988 (poem revised).

FIVE GREAT GIFTS

And a prophet of God's message
Stepped forth to sing praise for
Five great gifts of life. And he
Spoke thus for each listener's
Heeding:

"**Share** of yourself with a special
Other,
Create new life from love with
Another,
Care for and nourish the young,
Develop your common and special
Talents fully, and
Share your talents with the
World."

Reprinted: Harper's *Romantica: On Peace & Romance*, 1988.

RENFRED*

This is my heart,
This is my soul,
This is the blood of
My blood—
The blood of God's flow
Of life through me.
This is the gift of His light
Bestowed; His light on me and
My woman love of life.
This is my heart,
This is my soul, my future untold,
My presence to behold;
This child is my son,
This child is our son,
Our life, our love,
Our shining light,
Our breathing soul,
Our precious gift as God's trustees
Of His life—
As God's trustees to create life.

The name Renfred means peacemaker. It is derived from the Teutonic or old Germanic language.

THANKS TODAY

In case I am not here tomorrow,
I say thanks today;
Thanks for good family, friendships,
And all kindness to me;
Thanks for well-wishers and supporters
Along my path;
Thanks for life's beauties of land, sea,
And air;
Thanks for the many smiles, encouraging
Words, and helping hands;
Thanks for all gifts and expressions of
Love;
Thanks for the universal God and
Benevolent spirits that watch over me;
In case I am not able to be here tomorrow,
I say thanks today.

Reprinted: Harper's *Poems on Love & Life*, 1985.

THANK YOU GOD

I bend a knee in grace,
And lower my head with face,
To thank my God today.

I bend my knee and pray
This day, to thank my God
For His celestial spirits that
Watch over me,
For His guardian angels that
Protect me.

Thank You God,
For all that You have blessed
Me to do and be;
Thank You God,
For allowing me the insight to
See Your grace along my path—
To see Your light from day to day.

AMEN.

AMONG THE GREATEST THINGS

The greatest reality is
Our existence here on Earth;
The greatest resource is
Our ability to create;
The greatest capacity is
Our capacity for love;
God's greatest gift to us is His
Gift of life and a capacity to give;
Our greatest resource for good
Is God's shining grace upon us.

A GIFT TO YOU

A gift to you
For what you've done,
Not for what I expect of you;

A gift to you,
For what you are,
Not for what I want you to be;

A gift to you,
For what we have shared,
And not for what we give
To each other.

Reprinted: Harper's *Romantica: On Peace & Romance*, 1988.

GOD'S GIFT OF A LIFE

I have been blessed
Again to see the
Light of God shine
Once more upon my face
Through the gift of
Life itself in the smile
And joy—
In the scent of freshness
And the spontaneity of life alive—
Through my God's love and me;
We have been blessed
As one in a single instance of
God's miracle of creation;
We have been blessed
As one to see the
Light of God shine
Upon our faces
Through His gift of
Life itself in the smile
And joy of a child—
In the scent of our baby's freshness,
Innocence, and spontaneity;
Thank you God for investing in
Us to be trustees of Your creation—
Of life itself.

GOD'S GIFT

If I can give the world a gift,
Oh how I would;
If God blesses me as might be
To give a gift witnessed and accepted,
I surely would as maybe I could;

If I can give a gift
So one can simply see the seen,
And hear the heard,
Or sense the scent of God's life alive;
Then I will;

If I can give a gift
That is simply shown and presented as known
To one who's blind to see the truth of His Spirit,
Then I will;

If I can give the world, or one within, a gift
To see through sculpted words of God through me,
Then I would, as I believe I could;
If I can give the world or one within the gift
Of wisdom within oneself to know God's gift—
That gift of good to share and touch the world;
Forever, to touch another's life,
To touch another's world—
Then, certainly, I should.

GOD'S POETRY

There is no training
    For the writing of good poetry;
It is a gift from the
    Spirit of God.

A poet of good is a conduit
Of God's message, a prophet
Of song whose gift must be sung
    Or it not be given more.

There is no training
For the writing of good poetry;
It is God's song to the messenger;
It is God's message to His
    Listening people.

Reprinted: Harper's *Romantica: On Peace & Romance*, 1988.

Frederick Douglas Harper

SPIRITUAL INSPIRATION

Frederick Douglas Harper

YOU CAN CHANGE

If you can believe in yourself,
Your inner spirit and soul can have power
Over the body that houses you.

You can change, if you will change;
You can do what you want to do;
You can do what you must do.
If you gain control of yourself,
You can be in control of your destiny.

So, seek strength from God's spirit
Within you;
Seek strength from God's spirits that can
Come to you and watch over you;
Seek strength in your power to change
Your thoughts, your attitudes, your feelings.

If you believe in yourself,
And the powers within, above, and around you,
You can change;
If you choose now to believe in yourself,
And the powers within, above, and around you,
You can change; you can change now.

IF YOU BELIEVE IN YOU

If you believe in you,
God's spirit can have divine
Power over what you do—
Then you can change;
Then you will change,
If you control the self you are,
You can determine the future you make;
If you control your mind and soul,
You can confront pains of the past
And challenges of the present and future;
So change now, by
Living in the light of God's spirit, and
Walking in the path of your divine destiny.

LIFE IS AN OPEN DOOR

Life is an open door,
Open to our talents or closed forever;
Life is a highway running,
Or exited prematurely at will or by chance;
Life is seldom flat as a plain
Or straight as a chiseled arrow;
Life turns and dips with time and distance;
Nevertheless, life is an open door,
Open to a future untold, but to a future that
We can mold.

CONFRONTING THE FUTURE

L et us confront the future—
Not with our backs to darkness,
But our faces to the light of the future;
Knowing that we are vulnerable and frail,
But courageous in will and perseverance;
Knowing that we must
Love God's Earth,
As we love or should love ourselves.

Let us confront the future within us
And the future within our young—
Confronting and painting our future
As artists who are bold enough to be free,
And moral enough to be responsible;
Let us confront and compose beautiful music
Of our future, with a courage to make us free
And at peace with each other and ourselves.

Let us confront our future, the future,
With a sense for doing that which is right.

IF YOU CAN, THEN

If you can do more good
Than you do, then do it;

If you can be better
Than you are, then be it;

If you have the opportunity
To do the right thing;
Then do not hesitate.

GOD'S PRESENCE

I like to realize God's presence within me;
I like to feel the security of God's presence
Around me.

My prayers are my thoughts of His divine
Presence and good will;
My temple of worship of Him is His continual
Presence in my heart.

I want to realize God's ubiquitous grace,
Always, through the good He has
Allowed me to realize within myself.

Reprinted: Harper's *Poems on Love & Life*, 1985.

ATIONS AND IGHTS

The world can be better
   With positive cogitation,
Healthy self-stimulation,
Focused concentration,
Interdependent inspiration,
And occasional elation.

The world can be better
With less self-adoration
And more other fascination;
With less detestation and idolization,
And more daily spiritual appreciation.

Each of us can be better
With internal emancipation,
Anger and violent hesitation,
And regular peaceful meditation
In our own quiet sequestration.

So let us stand by right,
Avoid future fights,
Dance and sing to our heart's delight,
And try to love or ignore the troubled—
Despite their toothless and
Sometimes toothy might.

IF GOD MOTIVATES ME

If God and His divine spirits
Motivate me,
Then I will motivate you;
And if I motivate you,
Will you motivate me by
The good you do for yourself
　　And others?

FORCES BEYOND US

There are certainly forces
Beyond our senses or will to know;
Energies in our presence that urge
Us where to go;
And if obliged, seem to protect
Us even more.

CHANGE

You will change;
It always happens;
Your needs will change,
Your interests will change,
Your values will change,
Your health will change—
And so will your image.

Don't be too confident now
In what you have and are;
Just tentative, appreciative, and
Thankful for God's blessings
And gifts to you—
Thankful for what you are,
Thankful for what you have, and
Thankful for what you have become.

You will change;
It always happens;
You may have it
For today;
That's all anyone can say.

WE CAN: A MESSAGE TO HUMANKIND

We must believe in ourselves; and we must get others
   To believe in themselves if we are to make a difference;
Whatever we want to do, let us do it now;
What we choose to do, let us do it well;
Let us build new bridges that will lead us to
      Destinies unforeseen.
We can do so much, to have done so little;
We can do anything, we can do everything—
      If we only believe:
We can run 150 miles nonstop,
We can catch a speeding bullet in our teeth,
We can leap the width of a flowing river,
We can climb the tallest building like a mountain,
We can stop our heartbeat by concentrating
      On a single thought,
We can die and come back to life.
We are human being, a phenomenal machine;
If we can do all these things,
We can help another person.

Reprinted: Harper's *Poems on Love & Life*, 1985.

Frederick Douglas Harper

FAITH, MEANING, AND MISSION

IF YOU BELIEVE

If you believe in a connectedness
To a spiritual force beyond yourself;

If you believe in a relatedness to the
Sacredness of all life;

If you believe in the high responsibility
Of rearing right the young;

If you believe in the natural cycles
And balances of life's energy;

If you believe in a healthy respect for
The human race and Earth's habitat;

Then you believe in the God of all.

Reprinted: Harper's *Romantica: On Peace & Romance*, 1988.

FAITH

Find a purpose and believe;
Have faith in that Other
Than your others;
Believe in a spiritual source,
Believe in yourself,
Believe in your purpose,
Believe in your dreams;
Find a purpose within you;
Live and believe, in order
To live right.

Reprinted: Harper's *Romantica: On Peace & Romance*, 1988.

GOD'S PURPOSE IS MY PURPOSE:
A CONFESSION OF GOOD WILL

Let it be known that
I have tried to do the right thing,
And at times I have felt and been
　　Victimized by such,
While being accused of that attributable
　　To the accuser.
Let it be known that
I have tried to do the right thing,
And, at times, I have been vulnerable
To that not good of better judgment—
　　Especially in my earlier years.
Although not perfect as any,
I have tried to be better than I was on
　　Yesterday.
My goal has been to grow within myself
And share the fruits of my growth as gifts of God.
My purpose has been to help others to grow
In the same way that I have been
Helped and nourished by others of good;
The more I am persecuted, the more I am humbled
Within myself toward tolerance for human frailty;
The more I am blessed, the greater the burden of
　　Bearing well the cross of consequence
　　With good fortune.

ARE YOU THE MESSIAH?

A nd it was asked:

\-   Are you the Messiah cometh too?

\+   If I were, would I know,
    Or you expect me to tell you so?

\-   Are you the Messiah II cometh here
    To die for that which is true?

\+   If I were and knew, would I tell you,
    So as to void work to come by
    He Who is True?

MESSIAH II

L et a messenger
Step forth and claim a
Truth greater than self.

Let a messenger
Step forth and claim a
Purpose greater than self.

Let a messenger come
To save us from ourselves;
By preaching, by teaching—
The destined way,
The natural way,
The way of all goodness.

Let a true messenger
Of goodwill step from the
Herd to lead the flock
Of floundering masses adrift.

Let a messenger of peace,
Love, and respect teach
By word and example.

Reprinted: Harper's *Romantica: On Peace & Romance*, 1988.

A NAP

I took a nap
Without knowledge,
And awoke while still asleep;
Paralyzed and motionless but aware—
Knowing that God's spirit had spoken
A message conveyed,
Without my knowledge of it.

LOST TRAVELER

He often travels to meet many people,
Never likely to see again the eyes of
Faces unlikely again to see him.
Just recently, he traveled so and was lost
As to where he was;
When he asked a wise person as
To how to find his way;
She looked for the answer
Within his eyes;
And simply said:
"Wake up."

GOD IS LIGHT

G od is light, my light,
The light of my way;
I will not question His
Divine destiny shown,
Or the messages of
His angelic spirits whom
I have felt and known.
God is light,
My guide,
My way.

THE ESSENCE OF GOD

God created the universe, the stars,
The Earth, and all thereof;
God is the universe, the stars,
The Earth, and all thereof;
God is matter, energy, and motion;
God moves in us and is we;
God is all that is truly supreme
In time and in all space;
God has no beginning and no end—
God is infinity.

Reprinted: Harper's *Poems on Love & Life*, 1985.

GOD IS...

God is everything—
Time and space.
God is the infinite evolution of things—
Things ever changing.
God is things changing over time
And in space.
God is everything—
Everything is God.
God is life—
Life is God.
God is we.

Reprinted: Harper's *Poems on Love & Life*, 1985.

WHEN I'M DEAD AND GONE

When I'm dead and gone
Come visit my bones,

And say a prayer;

When I'm dead of me this life no more,

Continue to help the

World to see my plea

For them and Thee;

When I am no more

Of this Earth,

Plant a seed and nourish a tree;

Plant a seed and nourish a life

For Thee and me.

ONLY ONE

There is only one God,
The God of all That is All;

There is only one religion,
The natural way of respect for
All life and natural beauty;

There is only one type love,
True love that lasts;

There is only one race of people,
The human race;

There is one true happiness,
That of personal growth and fulfillment,
Purposeful giving, and personal peace.

A DISAPPEARING PRESENCE

There is a disappearing
Presence of God
In many hearts of His prized creation;
In many hearts of the human race.

There is a disappearing
Presence of love in the hearts and faces
Of many a man, woman, and child.

There is a disappearing kindness in
The ways of His human race;
Often, too many dash and pace in hectic
Haste, just to get a taste of
Status, power, glamour, riches, and pleasure—
But with emptiness and void of spiritual
Love, meaning, and the natural way of life.

RUNNING TO AND FROM

There are those who
Run because of tears,
And those who run out of fear;
There are those who
Will run because of greed,
Versus those who will hesitate in heed;
There are those who run because of lust,
Compared to those who wait for God's trust;
Then, there are those who remain
As humble as one could be,
Versus those who are corrupted
By their own pleasure and misery.

END OF A JOURNEY CONTINUED

When I come to the end of my journey,
I will not falter in the face of my curtain's
Fall, or exit from the stage of my destined call.

When I come to the end of my road
Shown clear, I will face death's claim
Without due fear, and look back, yes,
On a life well done, I will beacon
My spirit toward the light of the sun.

When I come to the end of this life's work,
I will smile in peace as I journey from
Earth; and all who would mourn me, I will
Bid them farewell, and trust in my heart,
They knew that I cared.

And when that day comes afar and not
Nearly, I hope to be in the company of
Those I love dearly; and with hands on
My loved ones and eyes toward my God,
I'll ascend from my body and head toward
The stars.

With faith in the future and good
Thoughts about the past, I will trust

That God's work will continue to last;

And as light will lead my soul to a

Place unknown, it is believed that God's

Work for me will continue to be done.

Reprinted: Harper's *Romantica: On Peace & Romance*, 1988.

SACREDNESS, ETHICS, AND MORALITY

Frederick Douglas Harper

A PLEA FOR RIGHT AND GOOD

As "good becomes bad,"
And as "bad becomes good,"
We need to take notice of
Such paradox;

As God and good become rebuked
In the eyes of the naively misled,
We certainly are in need to get
Down on our knees and pray,
Or suffer as a species one day;

As twisted values of right are
Replaced by aimless acts of
Malicious and egregious wrong,
Let us offer prayer of hope and
Actions of right and good;
Let us offer a plea to each other
To do what is right and good
Within ourselves, for ourselves,
And for God's sacred world.

LIFE IS SACRED

L ife is a divine creation of God's grand design;
Once conceived, it should not be destroyed
Except by its own decree to abort natality;
Once born, it should not be twisted, cheated,
Or snuffed out except by its own choice to
Deny self and others or by natural circumstance;

Life is sacred, life is precious,
Deserving of respect and owing respect;
Like a flower, let life bloom; like a star, let it shine;
Like a tree, let it seek its place among peers;

Life is sacred, life is precious,
But let no life preempt the integrity
And sacredness of other lives—
For they are also sacred and precious.

Reprinted: Harper's *Poems on Love & Life*, 1985.

TRANSIENCE OF LIFE

Life—so transient;
A bud flowered in spring
To be withered by its season's time.
A tree bared in autumn by
Each leaf's descent toward glory.

Hopes raised, dashed, and rejuvenated;
Cycles fixed but so limited by life's time passing;
Transience—precious moments fleeing
With each setting sun and its day's memories,
Memories that glow and fade with time gone.

Each sacred life, unique as God's creation—
Alive on Earth and then transformed
From that which we knew as once shared
And valued in its own space, time, and light;
Each unique life to appreciate in its transient state
As God's gift; each unique moment of life
To savor and to keep.

CRYING IN THE WILDERNESS

There are people who are
Crying in the wilderness;
Whose tears cannot be seen, and
Whose sighs cannot be heard;
There are babies drowning in their tears,
And Children crying out their lung's life.

There are people who are
Crying in the wilderness;
Whose sighs and sniffles can not go muffled;
Those who are often ignored, for they matter
Not so it seems to those
Who know not, care not,
Or fail to remember how.

There are people who are
Crying in the wilderness;
There are people who are the forgotten,
The ignored, the uncared, the homeless—
But of no less value in God's love.

PEOPLE ARE DYING

People are dying all around us,
 As time sweeps to destiny's fate.
Beyond the horizon,
Images of childhood
That preceded us
Have ascended, and
Spirits of yore linger in wait.

EARTH'S ANGER, A WARNING

When trees sing pain of wind's bruises,
And sun scorches deep the crust of Earth;

When Earth shakes and quakes its
Plates for days on and then no more;

When oceans spew pearls and debris from
Their secret depths of dark hidings asleep—
And life of land and sea bears for
Thee no more;

When we are no longer here to ask
When, what, where, or why,
Then Earth will once again
Be able to cleanse itself and live full again.

I AM VERY MUCH CONCERNED

I am very much concerned about
Those who fail to work,
But criticize the worker;
Those who do not victimize,
But lend no help to the victimized;
Those who do not victimize,
But stand by to watch the victimizing;
Those who fail to respect those who
Are respectable,
Or who drown the hopes
Of the hopeful,
Or depress the good energy
Of the excited.
I am very much concerned about
Those who would kill the spirit
Of the good-intentioned and talented;
Who would kill the spirit
Of those blessed by
God's gifts.

WHEN INCOMPETENCE
CONFRONTS COMPETENCE

When incompetence criticizes competence,
It is a time to pause for thought.
When incompetence continues to
Criticize competence, undeniably and unjustifiably,
Certainly, it is time to move;
It is time to move up or out;
It is time to move up to power and influence
Or out to peace, tranquility, and personal growth.
It is a time to move
Where one can be appreciated and
Where one can appreciate self;
It is time to move—
Where one can do God's work
At its best.

TOO WEAK TO BE STRONG

There are those who are
Too weak to lower their voices
Below a shout;
Too insecure to talk sensibly
To those whom they accuse, or
Too rigid to do the simple and
The expected.
However, let us beware that
Among these are those who are
Strong enough to reek havoc
Upon the stable and the well intended;
Strong enough to trigger the end of a
Good life.
For these persons, let us always
Have mercy;
For these persons, let us always have prayer,
While being aware and vigilant of their potential
For unnatural and untimely destruction
Of life, love, and peace.

ON PEACE, LOVE, AND NATURAL BEAUTY

Frederick Douglas Harper

ODE TO EARTH

All praise to God's universe
Of Sacred energy—
To His astronomical garden of flowers;
All praise to God's jewel, God's pearl;
All praise to God
For His divine and living Earth;
All praise to the sacred resource
Of us, our life;
All thanks for Earth's glorious stuff of life—
Its air, water, and soil;
Its divine mosaic of plants and animals;
Every praise to God's Earth—with its daily
Touch of His warmth as sunlight of our life;
All praise to God's Earth as our home,
As His home for us.

PEACE WITH EARTH

L oss of a life is unlike
Loss of the life of a species;
Loss of a human being is unlike
Loss of the human race—
A loss, an extinction from our own
    War against mother Earth.
Make peace we must or die we will
With Earth's air, water, plants,
    And animals;
Make peace we must with God's
Sacred whole or go we will
    The way of the dinosaur,
    The way of those which are
    No more;
Let us have peace with Earth,
Let us have peace on Earth,
Let competition give way to
    Cooperation,
And let existence give way to
    Coexistence.

Reprinted: Harper's *Romantica: On Peace & Romance*, 1988.

THE WHITE LIGHT

L OVE, PEACE, AND JOY;
Let us strive for these—
Let us strive for these in our
Hearts, our thoughts, and our
Actions.

Let us strive for the
"White Light" here on Earth
Through peace in the world,
Joy in our hearts,
And love toward one another.

Reprinted: Harper's *Romantica: On Peace & Romance*, 1988.

PEACE I

For every good deed done,
You will be blessed ten-fold;
Give and let there be peace;
Take and there will be unnatural destruction,
Destruction to you.

Let all warriors cease to fight unless fought;
Let all destroyers cease anger, hurt, and
Viciousness;
Let us avoid jealousy and hatred,
Greed for another's bread, and
Distrust of those who trust;
Let there be peace by being at peace.

Blessed be the man who walks tall in resisting
Destruction of self and his world;
Blessed be the woman who hoards not the
Treasures of precious stone, metal,
Fragrance, and fabric;
Let us enjoy life's natural fruits and consume
Not the entire vineyard nor destroy the
Countryside.

Reprinted: Harper's *Romantica: On Peace & Romance*, 1988.

LET THE CHILDREN BRING PEACE

A purpose of life is to create life,
A purpose of life is to nourish life,
A purpose of life is to respect the
    Sacredness of life,
A purpose of life is the perpetuity
    Of us—of the human species;
So let us shun violence, shame war, and
    Disdain human destruction;
Let our young foretell a future of love
    And peace through their innocence
    And precious hopes as our future;
Let countries and cultures exchange their
    Children's smiles, talents, and love
    Through their tiny voices and bright
    Faces, and through their joys of
    Word and song;
Let the children bring peace to our minds,
    Our hearts, and our world;
Let the children bring peace to their
    Future by our efforts with them.

Reprinted: Harper's *Romantica: On Peace & Romance*, 1988.

BEAR A CHILD

If you love one another,
Bear a child;
And let such
Test your bond with time.

If you love each other, create
God's life as trustees of life,
And test that love, your commitment,
Your manhood, your womanhood,
Your humanhood—
To do right for you and Him.

As you love each other through His grace,
Love a child through life's times and
In His grace on you to bear His fruit of life.

MIRACLES OF CREATION

Miracles are molded from
Divine events with time, and by
Time vested in right for the molded;

God so exists because we exist,
With and among the splendor
Of myriad miracles;

As the miracle of our own creation
Unfolds, learn we will, more about our
Origins as we ascend to destiny's pull;

God, as creator of us within His being,
Has given us that entrusted potential
To create ourselves, our futures,
Our own possibilities for miracles as
Trustees of His divine work of art.

ODE TO A FLOWER

Oh flower, in the light of sunshine
And the secrecy of night's cover,
Show your beauty;
Show your beauty through the moisture
Of dawn's dew and the teardrops
Of April's rain;

Oh flower, the source of a florist's
Dream to create your gift for
The giver's gift of love and
Compassion;

Oh flower, a flower;
The repeated miracle of God's grace
Through the arms of plants so green
With outreached blossoms for life's
Touch;

Oh flower, smile for me;
Oh flower, smile that we
Might see the love of Thee.

Reprinted: Harper's *Romantica: On Peace and Romance*, 1988.

IF TREES COULD DO AS WE...

If trees could talk as we,
Oh, how they would echo
    Earth's praises;
If trees could sing as we,
Gee, how they and we would
Harmonize a sweet song of
    Spring breezes;
If trees could walk as you and I
With dances of lift and light;
If trees could, then we could
Imagine of them, their life, their soul,
In our minds and hearts;
And spare of them their life for us.

GOD'S SUN, GOD'S LIGHT OF LIFE

Light of the Earth,
Light as our light,
Light as our life;

Shine, oh shine on us;
So we may see that light
Of our life, God's light;

Shine, oh shine on us;
So we may see
The light of God around us, and feel
The warmth of God within us.

THE SIMPLE LIFE

I want to go where
Life is simple;
Where breezes blow against
Willowy blades of green,
And sun rays sprinkle blankets and
Mounds of grassy knolls and hills.

I want to go to the countryside,
And breathe breaths of life's force—
And smell life itself in every
Simple and sacred form.

I want to go by the seashore
Where rivers flow and see the fishes
Galore, you know;
And one day surely, I'll do just that;
And ask for little else and no more.

I CRY WITHIN MY SOUL

When I look at the trees
  Of autumn and flowers of spring,
  I cry of joy within my soul;
I cry within my soul with joy
    When I turn toward the face
    Of a child with a smile,
    Or see the golden sunrise at dawn,
    Or the moon in full bloom at dusk,
    Or the stars bright at night,
    And the bees and birds in flight,
    Or the winter snows, cool rain's pour,
    And refreshing wind's blow;
Why is it that I cry within my soul's eye?
    It's simply because I realize and
    See that life is much more than
    You and I.

Reprinted: Harper's *Romantica: On Peace & Romance*, 1988.

THOUGHTS ON SPIRITUALITY

(Original Quotations of the Author)*

Time is truth; everything else is insignificant.

«««

Since we often cannot hide the truth, it may be good policy to admit it or to say nothing.

«««

We tend to choose our past by determining our future; and those misfortunes we did not or could not control, we should try and simply forget or ignore.

«««

When you create something good, some people want to use it; when you do something that is good, some people want to use you.

«««

True love is a locked love of commitment that will not let go of itself unless both persons involved agree in kind or as God wishes.

«««

The loss is greatest when the hope is highest.

«««

Those who allow themselves to be pulled by God's destiny's force, themselves, become a pushing force for positive changes in others.

«««

---

*Some of the quotations within this section were reprinted from F.D. Harper's *Poems on Love and Life* and *Romantica: On Peace and Romance.*

I have traveled much, I have seen much, and I have read much; and I would like to think that I am much better than I would have been otherwise.

《《《《

To handle loss, one must first understand that he or she cannot own.

《《《《

A person who is destined to shine cannot be kept in the dark.

《《《《

As messengers, we cannot profess to be immune from the news of the message.

《《《《

There are those who are chosen and those who choose themselves.

《《《《

We very often long for that we leave.

《《《《

One has to be inspirational in order to inspire, and one has to be "inspirable" in order to be inspired.

《《《《

There surely are those who don't want to be in charge, but who want to take charge.

《《《《

Evil forces are sometimes more cohesive than forces of good, because often the main motive of evil forces is greed.

《《《《

If we cannot live right as "human beings," we will surely and prematurely die as a species.

《《《《

As a way of life, we should always carry our religion in our heart, and our prayers we should always carry in our thoughts.

《《《

The perpetuity of love should be every day, all day, more and more, and in every way.

《《《

There are those who seize success, and there are those who take advantage of the success of the successful.

《《《

People who have nothing for which to look forward, very often spend much time looking backwards.

《《《

You cannot take away a shared time or a shared experience; you cannot take away a pleasant memory of love.

《《《

Among all things of value, one should try to be true to oneself and true to one's purpose and mission.

《《《

We tend to go *along* and be *alone*, until we meet someone special or experience something special.

《《《

Power is what some people "live for," and power is what some people "die for."

《《《

We cannot change our memories of the past, but certainly we can shape future memories through shaping our future experiences. We cannot change out memories of the past, but sometimes we can change our perceptions about these memories.

《《《《

Where change does not occur by will, it is, unfortunately, likely to occur by force.

《《《《

Some persons would rather be right than do right.

《《《《

A man should like a woman as a person before he loves her as a woman; a woman should like a man as a person, before she does likewise.

《《《《

It's not how far you get off course but how soon you get back on the right path.

《《《《

Boys need men in order to learn how to become men. Boys need men in order to keep from attempting to be men before their time.

《《《《

We may sometime have to part from that we love because of a greater love for ourselves, or because of a greater love for God's purpose.

《《《《

For those things we cannot figure out, we must simply accept.

《《《《

Don't talk too quickly to one who is deep in thought, because that person may very well be talking to oneself.

《《《《

The greatest love is the sacrifice or sharing of self for the happiness, welfare, and growth of another human being. It *is not* selfish gratification from the neglect or misuse of another human being.

«««

Conflict is a child of pleasure and surely sometimes its mother.

«««

With every blessed success, it is wise to keep your feet on the ground, but not in the mud.

«««

Although we may see ourselves as an oak in our conscious state, we can very often be a weeping willow in our sleep of raging anxiety and nightmarish thought.

«««

If you stick around "good" people, you tend to get better, and, if you stick around "bad" or destructive people, you are very likely to get worse.

«««

We all have a script written for us; that is, if we only follow it—if we only follow our hearts and God's angelic spirits as our guides.

«««

The purpose of human-made science, so it seems, is to destroy Earth's life while attempting to save it.

«««

I sometimes wonder how I will die; but even more, in my wondering, is how I should live.

«««

The simplest purpose of life is to survive and to recreate life.

«««

Unfortunately, some persons don't marry the one they love, and some don't love the one they marry.

«««

One of the greatest gifts is the gift of one's time to another.

《《《《

Some things are too painful to relive in the mind, and are often better forgotten if they bother us not.

《《《《

Sometimes, while we are thinking about whether something is worthy of having, someone else gets what we are thinking about while we are thinking.

《《《《

There are those who talk too much and too long about nothing.

《《《《

When you can't control the situation, you have to try to control the impulse.

《《《《

There are those who live for a good cause, and those who take advantage of a good cause.

《《《《

Man can plant a tree, but only woman can bear its fruit.

《《《《

It's good to be good, but it's better to be better.

《《《《

Try to give for the gift of giving, and try to receive in the spirit of appreciation.

《《《《

There are many special people who have yet to realize that they are special.

《《《《

The purpose of destiny's glow is to stay in the light and flow.

《《《

Often people who do not demand respect are those who do not deserve it.

《《《

It is not so much a time to attack evil as much as it is a time in which we must promote compassion, right, and good.

《《《

Power rests within itself and within us. It is to be used and not abused.

《《《

There are few blessings without the burdens of responsibility, jealousy, and tests of patience and tolerance.

《《《

We acquire eventually to give and not to keep.

《《《

Try to judge people by their relationship to you and others, and not by what others say about them to you.

《《《

Those who follow on their knees, may one day find it difficult to lead on their feet.

《《《

Those who are rich in the gift to give will be rewarded by the appreciation of those who are recipients of their gifts.

《《《

Nowadays, there appears to be no privacy, except in our minds, our thoughts, and our fantasies.

《《《

Some people seem not to like people nearly as much as they need them.

《《《

Those who give much, tend to get back more, and those who try to get or keep too much, often lose what they've been able to acquire.

《《《

Pain makes us philosophical about purpose and essence; wherein pleasure makes us comfortable with our own selfishness and anonymity.

《《《

Our ability to raise the right questions is much more important than our intelligence to discover answers.

《《《

In our daily work, there are those whose company is surely not worth our energy; for they very often can prove to be more headaches than help to both themselves and us.

《《《

If you continue to be good to yourself, life will be good to you.

《《《

Always hope and plan for the best and be prepared for the worst.

《《《

In our thoughts, dreams, and choices, we can always be free.

《《《

It is not so important what people tell you, but, even more, what they *do not* tell you as well as what they ask you.

《《《

I should always try and remember to take no real credit except to carry out the God-given destiny within me and to realize the gifts blessed upon me.

《《《

You cannot help a person without being helped by that experience; you cannot willingly hurt a person without being hurt yourself.

《《《

Let us forgive those who are capable of forgiveness and let us love those who are capable of love.

《《《

If you leave some jobs, you can lose your health insurance; and if you stay on some jobs, you can certainly lose your health.

《《《

Some have the distasteful habit of berating the dead in order to advance the causes of the live.

《《《

I believe in "doing good" for no other reason than its effect.

《《《

At least two things are bad for the stomach: eating too much and eating too often.

《《《

Nowadays, we seem to put too much emphasis on freedom of choice and not enough on obligation of responsibility with choice. We seem to put too much emphasis on freedom of the individual and too little emphasis on freedom and rights of the group.

《《《

You can't get the spirit unless you seek the spirit; you can't seek the spirit unless you let it come within you.

《《《

If we are fortunate to be fortunate, we should help the unfortunate, that is, as long as we are not misfortuned by the unfortunate in doing so.

《《《

We are often so busy putting out brush fires, we do not have time left to plant a tree.

《《《

The seeds of truth blow not far from the tree.

《《《

Patience indeed is virtuous, that is, when it is not foolish.

《《《

We don't always have to remember in order to do things out of memory; that is, going many times to places we have been before and doing many times things we did or wanted to do before in another life or phase of our life.

《《《

If one wants to kill you for disagreeing with his or her religion, then that person is not religious.

《《《

Excellent students of yore and nigh tend to compliment their former professors for their successes in life, when the credit is mainly theirs; while students of lesser academic achievement tend to compliment fully and solely themselves.

《《《

The world is not simple any more, so we have to simplify it for ourselves.

《《《

We should love life, for life is God and all sacred energy within.

《《《

Special things are few, and special moments are often brief.

《《《

If we are special, then let us be special—let us act in a special way.

《《《

A key to happiness is to think happy thoughts, plan for happiness, and choose the company of happy people.

》》》

Many a people tend to hate that they don't understand and to want that they have not had.

》》》

Privilege is not a license for arrogance, and arrogance doesn't necessarily earn privilege.

》》》

Hope without action is futile thought.

》》》

A purpose of our spiritual life is to free God's spirit within us in order to move the good spirit within others.

》》》

By helping another, we help ourselves as two.

》》》

You can't come aboard and wreck a ship without the risk of drowning yourself.

》》》

People often try in public to be more grand than they really are.

》》》

Many a talented Bourgeois very often dream and talk of doing much in a lifetime, but tend to do one thing; that is, to maintain a style of life to which they have become accustomed.

》》》

We must work on helping people after our death; only then will our spirit live in kindness and perpetuity.

》》》

People surely should take an interest in other things besides themselves.

《《《《

There are people who watch things happen, there are others who let things happen, and there are those who make things happen.

《《《《

You find happiness wherever it is, and you embrace it; you trust in it.

《《《《

If you find out who you are and accept who you are, then you can become all you can be.

《《《《

Those who should be happy for you, can very often be jealous against you.

《《《《

Every good thing we are and become, we owe to God and His helping angels and spirits along our way. The only credit we can rightfully claim is that of being willing to listen and follow through with the divine script in trying to become and do all we can.

《《《《

The more we are blessed, the greater the burden and challenges that accompany our joys; because blessings are not without the price of intermittent setbacks, frustrations, disappointments, and pain.

《《《《

Persons who acquire a large sum of money all at once, should first cry, then keep their mouth shut and pray, and finally hide; that is, before deciding how to use it wisely.

《《《《

Those who deserve better should not seek nor settle for less.

《《《《

Those who try to do good things can sometimes be criticized for their efforts, while those who choose to do nothing are often simply ignored.

《《《《

It is not wise to think something is "one thing," but to know in our hearts that it is quite "another."

《《《《

Among other things, violence is often the results of anger's hurt and pain unleashed.

《《《《

Some people are at a dead-end street and are afraid to make a U-turn.

《《《《

Happiness comes within the privacy of its recipient, and sometimes with the presence and sharing of those loved and respected.

《《《《

Persons who are afraid of losing love will often not seek to gain it.

《《《《

As in yesteryears, we as human beings have brilliant thoughts and artistic creations; however, nowadays, it seems we have fewer people who take time to appreciate these.

《《《《

One does not have to "sell out" just because he or she "buys in."

《《《《

We can often become victims of that we criticize.

《《《《

There are those who dig a hole deeper and deeper for themselves instead of filling in a small hole and starting to build a mountain.

《《《《

Sensual pleasure is something that lasts for a moment, romance often lasts for a season; but true love endures for a lifetime or more.

《《《

An alternative to being suspicious about good is that of being appreciative of good.

《《《

Always look forward into the light and not backwards into darkness.

《《《

We frequently admire in others the things we cannot do or the things we are afraid to do.

《《《

You don't have to be competent in order to recognize incompetence; nevertheless, it surely helps.

《《《

People don't just grow old; they allow themselves to get old.

《《《

Dying becomes less dreadful to those who have chosen to live.

《《《

There are some people who are driven by two forces, the need to gain status and the fear of losing it.

《《《

People will often act human if they feel they can.

《《《

When you motivate others, you are, in turn, motivated by what they do.

《《《

A gift that is well appreciated by the receiver is, in itself, a gift to the giver.

《《《

Remember and appreciate what you have been blessed to have, instead of being obsessed with that you have lost or not yet gained.

《《《

I remain amazed at the work that has to be done on Earth, but I am equally amazed by how some people stand or sit around doing nothing.

《《《

You don't have to know how to play the game in order to know it is being played on you. But if you participate with the game player, certainly, you stand a chance to lose in the process.

《《《

Every person is an opportunity; that is, an opportunity to be helped and an opportunity to help.

《《《

Human behavior can vary across settings and time, although basic traits are surely constant and many times predictable.

《《《

If you shine, then the light will reflect to you in the smiles and joys of others.

《《《

Those who make a positive difference will often benefit from it.

《《《

People who take responsibility and leadership, very often find little time to complain.

《《《

There are those who often look for others to criticize, as long as it is not themselves.

《《《

There is a tendency of those who knew us "when" to continue to see us as then.

«««

Butterflies are born to fly; it often matters not where or why.

«««

It should not be assumed that a person knows or even can know everything; however, it can be assumed that one should know that which is expected of him or her.

«««

If we know who we are, then we don't have to try to be.

«««

Every conversation is an opportunity for the good we can do.

«««

Give some people an education, and they will often use it to avoid work.

«««

Beyond sensual love is spiritual love; a love of knowing without knowledge, touching without hands, and being without trying.

«««

If a ship does not sink, it will inevitably continue to float; and if it floats, then there is hope.

«««

When a man can talk with a woman about things other than the obvious, then he is truly a gentleman. When a woman can listen to a man without prejudging a motive within him, then she is truly a lady.

«««

Your status, high or low, does not make you right or wrong; it is usually your action.

《《《《

As regard to retirement from a job, there is never a good time in which to leave, but there is always a good time in which to have to leave.

《《《《

Selfishness and righteousness should not occupy the same breath or the same space.

《《《《

Confused sheep will often follow any shepherd.

《《《《

At times, someone has to take charge in moving the ship ahead or putting the ship back on course.

《《《《

There are people who worship other people, when they often think they are worshipping God.

《《《《

A great power within any one person is to know and to realize such.

《《《《

Divine knowledge comes without effort; it is simply observed and accepted.

《《《《

Some people often far exceed their own expectations, not to mention the expectations of others.

《《《《

Although educable, human beings are among the most difficult animals to train.

《《《《

For some people to love another person, that other person would have to be "perfect" and more.

«««

A man who loved a woman before, should, once she is pregnant, love her even more.

«««

We don't necessarily need to reinvent the wheel; often we just need to make it roll.

«««

There will always be lies, but let them fall harmlessly upon the shield of truth and the sword of virtue.

«««

In one's brief lifetime, there is too much work to take time to dwell on the negative, and, certainly, too little time to criticize the insignificant.

«««

Unfortunately, level of motivation is not necessarily correlated with level of education.

«««

No social group has a premium on indolence; it can be found at all social levels and among all cultural groups.

«««

It is bad to fight with another, but it is even worse to be at war with oneself.

«««

God helps those who help others, and we can very often help others when we help ourselves.

«««

There are those who love most those things that will kill them quickest.

《《《

People who do absolutely nothing, often stretch the value of zero.

《《《

Some people love to see their names and faces in the spotlight, but they very often do not want to perform.

《《《

There are too many who want those they idolize to be bigger than they really are, while daring them to accept or espouse the exaggerated image attributed to them.

《《《

We often make some people angry by simply doing what is right, while we can make others angry by either doing what is wrong or doing what *we think* is right.

《《《

To want to be bigger than God and to want to be accepted as a God are two of the most selfish things one can do, because God is all and one person simply cannot be all.

《《《

We are often so busy assessing what's wrong with a person, we very often fail to see what's right with that person. We are often so busy looking for differences between a person and ourselves; we very often fail to see the similarities.

《《《

Death is not necessarily an ending; it's likely to be another beginning in life's energy cycle.

《《《《

It's always good to be flexible; as long as one does not break, as long as one does not shamefully genuflect.

《《《《

Personal growth can simply be defined as the forward progress from where we were and who we were.

《《《《

Those persons who grow little are often impressed by the least.

《《《《

Positive action results from positive thinking; positive action results from positive living.

《《《《

Most human beings have the vulnerability to be corrupted. All that is needed is the right opportunity. Most human beings have the inclination to be good and do right. Likewise, all that is needed is the right opportunity.

《《《《

Some people have nothing important which they choose to do, so they choose the constancy of trying to make a positive number negative, that is, trying to make good people look bad.

《《《《

Neither love nor anger can flourish in a vacuum.

《《《《

The truth often rests between two stories of opposing viewpoints, or it simply rests within the mind of the observer.

《《《《

If you don't expect anything, you don't have to worry about getting anything. If you don't expect anything, you won't set yourself up for disappointment.

《《《《

We never know our power until we have to use it; and, sometimes, we never know our power until we lose it.

《《《《

One who inherits the house is certainly responsible for cleaning it.

《《《《

We give our best to the best in order to avoid their being less than they could become.

《《《《

One can only go around in circles with success as long as the circles are concentric circles.

《《《《

There is only one way to avoid making mistakes; that is, to do nothing. There is only one way to avoid personal growth; that is, to do nothing.

《《《《

Every day is a curtain call, and we have to play well our role of living.

《《《《

We should not live to win wars, but, if anything, to win battles. And if we have to retreat, we should. And if we have to stand on the sideline and not fight a given cause, then we should—because, at times, wisdom is a greater virtue than courage.

《《《《

A good sensation lasts but a moment; however, a good thought can last a lifetime or more.

《《《

One should be defined less by position in life, but more by his or her work in life or work during a lifetime.

《《《

If we speak truth, we can often defy those we know best. If we do not speak out of truth, we can very often defy the very principles inculcated within the marrow of our bones.

《《《

Many can provide ideas, but few among these are willing to or capable of carrying them out.

《《《

We cannot change the past, but we can change our perceptions of it.

《《《

Sometimes, it seems there are so many people who are unhappy, that it is hard to find someone with whom to share one's happiness.

《《《

Everyone has a God-given gift or talent. Each must realize what it is, develop it, and then share the fruits of it with others. Failure of either of these is a loss of the most serious magnitude.

《《《

One purpose of a parent is to protect the life of the young—even if it is with one's own life, because the future life of a child is one's life continued; it is God's life continued.

《《《

Those who do difficult things by choice will find difficult things less difficult to do.

《《《

People who victimize others often self-exonerate by blaming their victims.

《《《《

Teach a child to do what he or she can do as a child, and that child will do what he or she must do as an adult.

《《《《

Those who work hard for the purpose of good, at times, must live with two challenges: negative criticism and lack of appreciation.

《《《《

Some things are good to have, some things must be had, and, even more, other things are best left alone.

《《《《

Some things are meant to be, but not necessarily meant to last.

《《《《

To avoid pain, one has to avoid the stimulus that causes pain; nonetheless, some pain is necessary for security and growth.

《《《《

Many people are frequently impressed by those with money, power, riches, fame, status, glamour, and prominence. Many people are frequently impressed by those who are said by others to be greater than their achievements.

《《《《

As human beings, we tend to be governed by our belief system. Anything outside that system is very often viewed as unacceptable, offensive, and intolerable.

《《《《

The further away we get from our natural way and state as human beings, the closer we will get to our death as a species.

《《《《

No nation at continuous war against itself can prosper.

《《《《

Where there is one, there is likely to be two, and where there are two there is likely to be many. If an event occurs once, it is likely to occur many times over, in many forms and variations, and in many places. Only God is one, all, and ubiquitous.

《《《《

That which is acceptable is very likely to be that which is popular in thought and preference.

《《《《

We often spend our early life trying to find out what we like, and, if we are fortunate, we will spend our later life knowing and enjoying what we like.

《《《《

Many times, it's lonely at the top and at the end of life, but it doesn't have to be.

《《《《

In aging, the key is to do it naturally, peacefully, healthily, and gracefully while functioning within one's own limits.

《《《《

Death of a loved one brings out grief and sometimes it brings out greed.

《《《《

Where there is a valued gift, there can be great joy; and where there is regretful loss of a valued gift, there can be sadness and grief.

《《《《

If you hate yourself, you are likely to destroy yourself. If you destroy yourself, you will likely hate yourself even more. If you cease to be angry, you can possibly begin to love and accept yourself.

《《《《

As life on Earth lives and dies, the Earth, itself, in time, will die.

《《《《

If you have peace and joy, relish in it and spread it to others; if you have pain, try to absorb it, flow with it, and tolerate it with time's passing.

《《《《

True friendship takes time, but, nowadays, people seldom find time for themselves, not to mention time for another.

《《《《

Some people very often brag that they can do something better than someone else, especially when they actually don't have to do it.

《《《《

Persons should strive to live in the light of the Greatest Spirit, because worship at a temple or church, *only*, "is not enough."

《《《《

If we continue to be so disrespectful to all life and ourselves and so destructive to natural things and ways, then death as a species will be a destiny that is earned but one that will not be necessarily deserved.

《《《《

It is very discouraging to often think that some too many do not realize when they are being helped and for what reason.

《《《《

These days, it seems there are so many things from which to choose, that we barely know what to choose to do with ourselves and our lives.

《《《

There are those who will take credit away from those who should be credited, and who will criticize those who are in a position to be the critic.

《《《

While corners of the world undergo pain, there are those of power and those of wealth who sit and pontificate in a corner of obscurity and self-indulgence, that is, while in a position to help.

《《《

When one does not appreciate the level of expectation of a teacher, one cannot realize what is attempted to be taught; when one does not care to learn, one will try but so hard.

《《《

It is easy to find criticism, that is, when you choose not to like a person.

《《《

Pain and misfortune are blessings if they serve to strengthen the soul and the spirit, that is, when they do not serve to destroy faith and will.

《《《

Religious leaders can be trained; however, true spiritual leaders are born of good deed and purpose. Nonetheless, religious leaders can be true spiritual leaders anointed by God's good spirit.

《《《

Sameness and repeated exposure can lessen appreciation; these can also, in many cases, enhance appreciation.

《《《

Everything claimed is not always earned, and everything earned is not worthy of claim.

«««

Unfortunately, everybody has done some things born of poor judgment and oversight.

«««

We cannot always write life's script as we think it should be, because God's spirit of hand is divine.

References

(complete references for reprinted poems and quotations from other works by Harper)

Harper, F. D. (1985). *Poems on love and life*. Alexandria, VA: Douglass Publishers.

Harper, F. D. (1988). *Romantica: On peace and romance*. Alexandria, VA: Douglass Publishers.

Frederick Douglas Harper

ABOUT THE AUTHOR

Frederick Douglas Harper has authored more than 300 published poems. As an international scholar and professor of counseling, he is author of more than 100 publications including college textbooks, journal articles, and book chapters. In addition, Harper has served as a professional counselor, university administrator, president of professional associations, and editor of two international, scholarly counseling journals. He has presented hundreds of motivational speeches and scholarly conference presentations throughout the world, including presentations in Argentina, France, Greece, India,

Ireland, the Netherlands, and Sweden. As related to this book's topic, Harper has presented numerous conference papers on psychospiritual counseling, and he has delivered scores of speeches in churches on spiritual living.

The author's most popular poem, "A Wedding Pledge," has been recorded on CD, recited in more than 5,000 faith-based weddings, translated into other languages, and reprinted in magazines. His poems have been read on WPFW Radio (89.3 FM) in metropolitan Washington, DC for more than 15 years, alongside the poetry and literary stories of the famous Langston Hughes. Harper's other poem books, sold throughout the USA and in numerous other countries, include *Poems on Love and Life* (1985), *Romantica: On Peace and Romance* (1988), and *Love Poems of Frederick Douglas Harper* (2003). The author has received hundreds of letters of appreciation and commendation on his poetry from readers of his work, including letters from public figures.

An extraordinary and highly spiritual human being, Frederick Harper has jogged more than 32,000 miles in 119 different cities throughout the world, and he has motivated and spiritually inspired many people through his writings, teachings, public speaking, and his way of life.

11/15/03

Gifts of Love I've
received -
1 - God's gift of me to my
parents.
2 - God's gift of a
husband + a daughter
3 - Gods gift to me of
brothers, sisters
nieces, nephews, family
+ friends
4. The florist lady
who always gave
me a big bag of
rose petals
5 - A gift of expenses
paid on moving
from NY to Va
by Ann + Diane
6 - Family remembering
me on birthday

6 - Celebrations of Birthdays
   & Anniversaries

7 - Free Rent (1 month)

8 - Basket of Appreciation
   from Housing Manager

9 - Free Taxi Ride's

10 - Luncheon by Hotel
    manager -

11 - Sincere Friendship
    by man.

12 -

13 -

Printed in the United States
1235700001BA/145-189